I0211997

WEAVING GREEN

Poems from a Tropical Farm

BY SUMI YAMAUCHI

copyright ©Sumi Yamauchi 2020

All rights reserved. No part of this book may be reproduced in any form by any means, electronic or mechanical, including photocopying, recording, or by any information storage or retrieval system without the express written consent of the author and publisher.

first printing, August 2020
ISBN 978-1-7354523-0-2

cover design and book layout, Limor Farber *www.limorfarber.com*

To read more poems, please visit poetreebird.com

poetree bird

This book is dedicated to my Father
who loved animals

Acknowledgements

Written especially for my dear goat friends who are no longer of this world.

Great thanks goes to all the animals and plants charming these poems into life --

To my Mother who joined in as editor and smiled at the poems, to my children who have always listened and cheered me in life --

To my grandmothers and grandfathers whose hands worked with plants, to all family and friends who have sat and listened to some poems or stories --

To all conscious farmers who plant seeds and boost soils, to Diana who encouraged and shared her enthusiasm for animal poems, to my dear friends Susie, Rieneke, who inspire me to keep writing --

To nature connection mentors John Young, Levon Ohai, Rosemary Gladstar and many others, to hellopoetry.com and friends inside for creating a poetry world --

To Gage for his sharp photographic eyes and Limor Farber for her fabulous wisdom and support in the process of self publishing. --

To the writing angels who guide my ink

and to Mother Earth for all her wisdom.

TABLE OF CONTENTS

The Herbivores

Other Farm Friends

The Birds

The Plants

It Comes with the Farm

Herbivores

 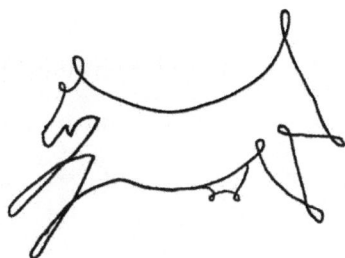

Starlight

Black beauty her first name
white star on her forehead
led her right to Gage's heart
he named her
he loved her
he milked her
laughed at her babies climbing
on her back
steadfast she chewed her cud
swelling her udder to milk us
into goat lovers

Amorita

We sang to her, Amorita we love you
Amorita we love you so,
Amorita Amorita we love you so

And we milked her
and tried and tried
and she kicked
and kicked and kicked

Till we had each of her legs-
even her head tied to
the milk stand

How ridiculous we all looked trying but
not getting milk from our dear Amorita

In the end, we retired her
and let her just be a goat

*Amorita, our first in the goat herd, taught us how to milk a goat,
and how to not milk a goat. We truly understand the statement
"stubborn as a goat!"*

Lancelot

Royal blood
pride and goat amble
your presence
gave all a feeling
of safety
Amorita your true love
To the ends of the
earth would you follow her
how you would perfume
yourself every day,
to attract every doe,
and make me laugh
and wonder
in the days of yore
how did men
naturally perfume themselves
every day to attract the gals?

Male goats naturally urinate on their "goat beards" frequently throughout the day, and then strut around, using the scent to attract the attention of the does. Say the word "goaty smell" and we know what this means!

Kiwi

I never understood
what a nursemaid offered,
until I met Kiwi,
watched her
become milk goat
simply by the presence of
the goat matriarch,
no need for pregnancy
her udder swelling
simply because
she was on the farm,
maybe she saw her mother Amorita
with all the kids—
human and goat
and wanted to give as well

*Kiwi was the last of the goat matriarch; she passed away May
2018. She lives on in our hearts forever.*

Tara

The weest of goats, most clever fence climbing, tree walking
buck loving doe, pregnant when only four months old

When her kids climbed the fence
into the buck pen, got pregnant
had kids as kids, we knew we had trouble on the farm!

Overwhelming to live in a goat multiplication problem
without natural birth control

We love her, do not need more of her,
so we relocate her plus her progeny

To a man wanting to add to his land
after subtracting his goats in a flood

So now Tara continues multiplying
as mother, grandmother, great grandmother
great great grandmother, great great great grandmother...

This goat so mischievous, she could make me
laugh and cry at the same time!

Java

Coffee black back like the midnight sky
eyes as blue as the sky at noon

Such a handsome bloke
with the attribute of horny as a goat
he bleats and sings of his yearnings,

And yet despite his artful scent dance,
to be smitten with them all

He never could quite deliver,
never sire, though sincere,
and, still he was lover, loved and beloved

Mango

If he were human
noble praise would have accompanied
him with his blue eye gaze
of sweet kindness

He was larger than the others,
black with white cherub blessings,
perhaps his heart had doubled
in size as well,
never a kinder gentler soul than he

I remember children
and adults of all sizes
just wanting to ride on him
and he would just let them, bareback

Always he would come to greet
and nibble with his tender lips
shoots of grass, leaves of ti

Sweet Mango
so sad you had to go

Mango lived the most years of all the goats, and touched so many hearts near and far with his sweetness. Sigh, we miss him.

Noni

Tricolored pinto goatling,
patient, loving, smaller than average wether

Running with the bucks
running away from the bucks,

Hiding in the herd, and arriving first
when the alfalfa and branch cuttings came
even though everyone wanted to butt

Peacemaker, son of Amorita
forever kind
innocent, intelligent,

Named after the medicinal fruit
though Noni the goat never smelled quite as ripe as
the smell of an over ripe noni

Buff

We buried Buff near the house
as requested by my son Ty, to keep him safe,
he, the first of the herd to die,

Young beautiful innocent buck
from the hands of a vet
who refused to read the book of goat,

I held in my hands reciting,
"Do not give any goat anesthesia, or they will likely die"
and because I did not stop him-

I am so sorry Buff

Feeding Time for the Goats

Sun rising, saliva stirring, tension rising
eyes and ears alert to crunching sounds,
footsteps carrying buckets of alfalfa
dragging limbs of gliricidia, hibiscus, areca palm, ti leaves
hooves shuffling for a spot on the fence,
dancing, butting , pushing, bleating,
me first, me hungry, me alpha
sweet nuzzling noses into hand as enter the gate,
pushing into the bucket
milk goats udders swollen and dripping
cat following despite goat butting
time to trade fresh food for fresh milk

Gentle Giants

Girth
like earth

Eyes
like stars

Muscles
like mountainsides

Hooves
like smooth stones

Stance
like towering tree

Appetite
like hungry garden

Face
shows unwavering truth

This horse
a world unto itself

Feeding Time for Horses

Cadence of clops, swishing of tail
brightness of eyes, bristling of mane
shifting of weight, lifting of chin
so many ways to say I am hungry
without a neigh

Grass Bowl

Blossoming horse cheeks
feathered mane
big eyes smelling life
nose aflame
long tail lashing
appetite flashing
silver light casting
on dark bronze matting
green pasture
beauty in a bowl
long live you horse
when you get a second course

Apparently all the grass that grows here, is absolutely the wrong nutrition for horses, hence feeding time offers the real nutritional feed.

Kaikane

In the far distance
herd grazing
calling his name loudly,

"Kaikane"
   "Kaikane"

Watching his shape
rise to my voice
gallop over hill and dale
across streams and stones
come right up to my side
eyes beaming bright
enthusiasm in his steps
makes me feel
needed, connected, and loved

Iherd

The mind of the herd
like the power of word

Can send a paragraph many legged
cantering towards greener fields

Or turn the pages to lean on fences
till reaching yonder pastures where
the dew shines oh so bright

Perhaps finish the book like what a
pasture looks like when the horses have read
each and every blade of grass

Maybe awaken the encyclopedia set
alpha leads the way, betas and the rest
soon to follow

In the mind of the herd
I heard those words

Freely Friesian

His soul a servant to the wind
mane bonded to currents sliding
through tall grasses

Tail and long fine hairs on legs spirit the breeze
tall standing outstanding
so brown his coat see purple and black

Hooves beyond fine teacups on the table,
rather like beer steins
on a sturdy farm bench

Yet fine and royal in his movements
yet grand and loving in his sweet eyes
this one speaks nurturing tidal waves

In his glances in his leans with full bodied head
and when the wind calls,
his spirit moves in horse gusto

Regal

Elegance in lifting hoof
As Clydesdale, large draft
horse towers above all
head can see yonder and beyond
his to and fro greater than
just the mere horse who he stands
near by and by
far and far great and great
sleek and regal stands he

Mermaid on Horse

I watched her father drop her off
on the dirt road, perhaps she had just left
the ocean and come to the fields

She promptly slid under fence
whistling to her horse,
who came running

Stacking two plastic chairs
one on top of the other
then throwing her surf leash over shoulder

The horse followed her eyes
to stand in front of the stack
clambering up, balancing, leaning forward

Grabbing mane bringing her tiny leg
over the horse's back
once on, swinging the surf leash back and forth

Until landing above horse's nose,
clicking her tongue, pulling her home made harness
bare backing into the hills and dale

Whistling to the other horses to follow
this merchild
so free, on land on horse

Do Horses Cry

My young son asked watching a tear drop
fall from the corner of Aria's eyes
her long white eyelashes batting
as I shared stories of her former owners
they no longer live here
we stood side by side as if two old
girl friends from long ago, yes
yes I think horses do cry I said
as a well of tears drew up in
mine eyes

Other Farm Friends

Having animals attracts more animals

Tale of the Tail

Resilient footprints cradling mud
earth embracing stories from last night
read the tracks, the trails, the tails
to find the tall, the tan, the thin, the claw,
the folk, the lore
the tale of the tail

Dogs Can Smile

Mine does, when he gets all the pets
and prances he needs

I've seen a few others raise the corner of their lips
generally to greet the favorite member of the pack

Though, not all dogs smile, only a special few

And, when he stops smiling for a long while
I can tell, he feels neglect

Farm Cats

First there was Makani, she blew in like the wind
loving people mice and rats, even those with fin

Then bestowed upon us, a special gift one night
kitten tangled in a crab net hanging on the wall

Earning her name her after the ama crab,
she never used her claws
she doesn't mind one year old Ko carrying her dragging
legs and tail

Ama Yeow and Socks came as a pair, one all black,
one black and white
rescued by a black lab, two cats became dog lovers

Mini kitten like a tiger wandering on road,
we picked her up a wild thing

And turned her into the most cuddly huntress ever born,
Shumba!

Message to the Farm Cats:

A rat a day makes a happy farmer

Huntress

Impossible to stop her claws
from coming out as she
hears new birds

Even the sound of her
meow, trembles, stutters
like the sounds of the birds

Oh she watches them
leaning into air, falling
to earth, flapping

With new feathers strong
they must learn fast or
fall prey to claws and teeth

In predator mind she
cannot give up the hunt
cannot stop her limbs from

Climbing up bark in pursuit
of fliers who do not know
about claws and fur and
hunger of the primal kind

When Dogs Eat Grass

I always heard it meant rain
I don't know what it means,
other than I know they like to eat grass

Turns out they like to eat lots of other things
I didn't imagine they'd like, lilikoi, flax seeds, avocadoes,
katydids, carrot bits, chicken poop

I see the cats do it too, eat the grass
so I got the kids to do it too, after all
all grass is edible

Can't die from grass, we can graze like horses
find a tall one, pull out the shoot,
chew the new growth

Buffalo grass the softest sweetest
most tender shoot, and try the others too
no reason to not think like a horse, a dog, a cat

Sometimes

The Rabbits

We never could name them, only because
our hearts feel change, feel loss
and naming means pet,
and pet means love and protect,

For you see, in our plan to eat locally
we recognize our carnivorous side,
so we decide to go for rabbit divine

Whiter than cloud, softer than feathers
sweetness, purity, peacefulness, innocence, shy
yet hungry, teeth never stop growing
powerful hind kickers, watch out

We let them explore the earth on excursions from hutch,
friends with the dog his nose burrowing into
the soft cotton like candy
while his tail wags joyfully nuzzling nature,

Starting so small,
pink marbles it seems,
and grow to fit their name, California Giants,

Harvest day near, hard to believe all those greens,
all the alfalfa, making them
steadily blossom in size—so table here, knives steady
dinner almost ready

An odd trick we saw
to rub harvested meat in baking soda
put in fridge for awhile,
takes away the gaminess

Two rabbits left in the rabbit hutch, the mother the father,
two children on the table, to children at the table
dinner divine

*We completed two cycles of serving rabbit divine, and then
listening to our hearts, we felt complete and had pet rabbits for
quite awhile.*

Homage to Roots

I don't recall how he got his name,
showing up in my son's arms, a naked newborn pig
we pick off the tics crawling over his bod,
for two weeks or more than a hundred a day,
definitely a dedication to have a pure pig

A friend brought him by, didn't know what to do with
this little pig lost his mom, so he thinks of our farm,
lonely babe, we bring him in our home,
naked diaper-less running on floor,
soft nose nuzzling, bright curious bond to our hearts

We ask at the beginning just to be clear,
knowing pigs grow continuously
like sunflowers responding to sunlight
perhaps destiny would bring him into our bellies?
so hard to imagine, too small too sweet

Easy to feed when so young
small handfuls from our meals,

well trained with the toilet and all, so he joins our
family inside and out, one with the gang,
eats with us, plays tag, sits on laps on couch

What a pet!

At two months he discovers his power to plow earth
with his nose, despite plant, rock or NO!
small digs first, they get bigger, and when he freaks out the
neighbors with his grunts and medium size,
his free range days over, now life behind bars.

So sorry Roots—you don't like the cage,
except for the five gallon bucket that comes once a day
to feed your endless hunger we head to restaurant each day
gathering leftovers galore you eat like a king

You always like rubs, pats on your left rib cage side,
then one day you slump, don't rise,
depression at the wired limits now- no time outside,
I see your sadness and realize it's time,

Outgrown cage, we bring out
guitar, voice and violin, sing songs to our hearts
to say the end is nigh

Next day, the bucket comes to give this last bit of love,
and sadly the gun goes off while he eats his grub

In this harvest I felt sure I didn't want to taste
all this sweetness and sadness what more could I take
then realize, how can I not savor one
who we love, and relish the essence of his being
and when tasting his morsel feel joy and relief
in each bite a richness, a kindness a love of a special kind,
a gift to our family,

Thank you Roots

Gecko Boy

Modern myth worth retelling even believing in

Twas told even as a babe, geckoes took a liking to this one
surrounding him on baby blanket, crib, following him
as he crawled, walked, riding his shoulder as he ran

Family and friends enjoyed watching this
unusual relationship then one day
while chasing the soccer ball into the road
a car could not stop, swiping him onto the ground

Ambulance came, carefully carying him
to the nearest hospital, family weeping
as news from the doctor came
to remove the leg below the knee
and so the doctor did

Later it happened as the young boy lay at home in bed
the geckoes came, in droves filling his room
as he rested and recovered for days, weeks, months

Then a miracle began to happen,
his leg began to grow millimeter by millimeter,
moment by moment, breath by breath
till longer came his limb, from ankle through to toes

And then he did come to run and play again
as all children rightfully should
and became known as gecko boy

How She Curls

Legs splayed wide she licks
her orange hairy belly with sandpaper tongue
meticulously cleaning, then onward to the outside
of the legs, curling in tight ball, and resting such display
of self love, this little cat shares how she cleans
how she curls, how she deeply rests

The Evening Parade

Hands that feed them, lead the parade
the cats, dog, goose, follow the lead
each threading into line
padding across grass, by the gardens,
down the hill

Oh the divine animal connection
walking in sunshine, skipping through drizzle,
this little evening parade, like a walking honor
homage to the hands that feed

The Birds

Wild and domestic, the blend

Dawn's Chorus

Darkness beginning to glisten-
sweet long high tweets stir into the rising glow
spreading melody from the low branches into the grasses,
solo sounds chime across landscape,

The roosters not the first ones
to wake the day
or act the loudest,

Rather the red headed cardinals
break the silence of the night
the contrast of their sweetness to the darkness
becomes louder than any sound I know,

The awakening dawn's chorus sings into the day
living inside heart and soul
ringing of peace

Put a Feather in Your Heart

Become like a bird
what?

Observe them, feel them
become them

Put a feather in your heart
they sing for space
they sing to bring in the sun
they sing to charm,

They sing to their lovers
they chat with their children
and each song they sing

Touches the soul of anyone who
has ears, a heart and a beat
be the bird you are
and fly, fly above it all

Hark to the Lark

This rain
ceasing singing
meadow lark's
brilliant high
notes brighten
the leftover
drizzle and
gray of this
morning waking
this singing
in the rain
this bringing
in the frame
this letting go of
all the old thoughts
down the drain

Red Bird

Mid day cardinal
trumpets trilling of
triumphic catch
in day so far
twelve bites papaya
fourteen roaches
one small sip of
banana tea forty
nine ants and one
fat worm while little
babes peep from nests
in chorus singing
feed me feed me
feed me now more
imploring
more more more

The Fledglings

Large pot hanging in outdoor kitchen
with steamer basket inside
pregnant shama bird sees this,
why not use as a nest she wonders

She and he carry long grass strands
wafting and weaving home inside the pot
does she not see the cats who prowl for rats
in this kitchen?

Mother shama bird burrows
in steamer basket keeping eggs warm
days and cups of teas later
bubbling sweet peeping starts
while pot boiling, do my best to not look
too close when the cats in the kitchen,
though, surely they must know

Parents fly in and out as
the naked ones soon grow downy fluff
when wings begin to show color
they fledge, I tuck the cats in the house,
to buy time

For new fliers, on ground time,
attempting jumps, flutters, takes a whole day,
tried and true, by nightfall I see them
on lower branches of monkey pod tree
survivors for this first aerial day

In Choir

I heard darkness
smiling last night
joyous crickets
raising the volume
of sweetness into
the air as if singing
to stars and beyond

Big dipper hanging
above ocean horizon
ladling cradling
the black of sky

This morning the
ecstatic cacophony
of bird song arriving
in my ears as if
birth itself in choir

Earth singing loud
to my heart swelling
with life's songs,
happy to be alive
yes happy to be alive

The Girls

The hens, called "the girls"
all acted pretty much the same-
see the white bucket, follow it around
see the greens, grains, grunge
beak to ground
cockroach coming, peck it
gecko running, grab it

Only one stood out,
brighter than the rest,
Silky her name,
she came running when called
fearless, calling her name, she came like
a heroine- running full speed
to nab the centipede in the path, her bravery
alas led to her meeting a wild dog

Troubles came, when the l'il mites
burrowed under feathers
blasting all girls covering them from head to toe
leading to a strong desire for sunshine and dirt baths
we built the chicken tunnel,

keeping them safe from wild dogs

they would crawl ninja style through

the caged tunnel into sunlight

away from the shadowy trees over their pen

and into the hen spa to bask in the fire of the day

The glory—

collecting eggs of all colors

dark brown, light brown,

speckled brown, blue,

the egg carton always looked

so unique, no two alike

Hoppy

There's some lore about the centipede
who tried to bite off her young chick leg
and in doing so dislocated her femur
giving her a gimpy style of hen hopping
around for her meal

Hoppy's gait troubled the other
hens, they pecked her mercilessly
and the rooster continuously power
played on her

So Hoppy lived away from the others,
hopping on the outside of the pen
making do with her one good leg

While her other one splayed sideways
like a ruler measuring the width of
her stride

I don't know how she survived the wild dogs,
pigs, and other roosters
patrolling outside the pen

She sat on eggs for the farm
she stood on one leg tending
many broods of baby chick,

She did her share of farm work
for a challenged chicken
I don't know how she lived so long

On her last days, her feathers
glowed like diamond dust
she hopped further than I had ever seen her go

I had to dig deep
in the grasses to find her
bring her back to her zone

And a few mornings later,
in her fifteenth year,
I found her in eternal sleep

*Hoppy became a heroine on the farm, taking care of eggs
needing hatching, and baby chicks. Even though her odd way
of moving around made other chickens want to attack her, she
somehow managed to find a place on the farm to outlive all the
average hens.*

Napoleon the Soccer Ball

At less than the height of a soccer ball
he stood with mini-rooster aggressions
mustering up his best "cock a doodle doo"

As all the slender femmes around him stood
above his eye gaze he could chase them, woo them
scratch the earth for them,

They just could not see him—
so to bring his power into balance
when we came to feed him,

Every step practicing fancy footwork
with Napoleon the soccer ball attacking our shoes
he would make his bantam screams

Then one day the tables turned, this game just had to end
"I am sorry if I kicked you, straight out of the pen
because Napoleon like a runaway soccer ball

Left the feeding field and ran and ran and ran

On our farm, people would give us animals, and we would generally take them in. My neighbor gave us this odd mini rooster Napoleon. I think he longed for his own flock of mini chickens, and so being with the large chickens never suited him. He stayed for a few months then one day left the pen running into the world.

Chocolate

Chocolate the rooster,
sweet young araucana,
curious with charisma,
kind, debonair, charming
with his harem of twelve chicks
he free ranged in style—til somehow,
his testosterone rose with all
the bitterness inside him
ruffian rooster wanted to cock fight all
even humans, why even the toddler
roaming the land, he had never dealt with
a human mother, who could no longer
see sweet Chocolate, so his habits
'came to a mighty quick end,
Chocolate, last seen in a soup we all ate
tasting bitter like chocolate,
and yet sweet like the sun
on a hot summer day

I always wondered why the demeanor of our wonder rooster
changed. Years later my sons told me that had tried to teach
Chocolate to swim. He sure didn't like that, I'm sure that was
why he became a bitter rooster.

The Habits of the Tropical Rooster

The tropical rooster not the first
to crow in morning here
maybe the loudest
maybe the pushiest,
but not the first
me thinks the tropical rooster
somewhat lazy, somewhat
slow, somewhat of a pushover
just letting other song birds sing
the morning wake up call
however, he does oddly like to sing
to the moon at night,
cock a doodle doo moony doody doo
not always liked by those who enjoy sleeping

The Gaggle

Of geese
acting in tandem when one honks
they all join in, when one eats
they all begin, each of these geese
distinct in personality

Roman, roman tufted, wise
benevolent, fearless, kind to humans
Nene, (named after the Hawaiian goose) Pilgrim goose,
jealous, pushy, needing to nip humans or cats

Pua, partner to Nene bashful, shy, wants to run away
if too much attention, Rosie, affectionate to Roman
does not even know humans exist

And CQ, cilantro queen, the one who stands out-
born from an egg in incubator,
when hatching, ten sets of human eyes staring
at him, no wonder, he acts like each of us, his mother

When he was born, searching for food, cannot find one ant
pillbug, or leaf he would eat, none would he have,

until we give him cilantro, he gobbles,

thus naming him cilantro queen

and shortening to CQ when we learn we do not know

difference between he or she in the world of birds

Bonding to us, as sweet gosling,

taking turns carrying him in a little purse, or sack,

so he didn't honk incessantly,

the other geese refusing him,

he lonely for his feathered friends,

we bathe him in the kitchen sink,

(much more fun than a rubber duck),

some time later CQ learning goose ways,

becoming accepted by his fellow peers

I can see how a gaggle of geese,

an appropriate name for—

such an interesting crowd

*We still have Roman, the sweetest of all the birds. He has out-
lived all farm animals, and is now 25 years old! He plans on
continuing to live until age 40. Rather lonely now, after spend-
ing time with the goats and rabbits no longer here, he chooses to
spend some time with the farm cats, dogs, and wild chickens.*

Sky Pirates

Reaching skyward
mountain peaks
press presence
into clouds while
iwas let wings lift
catch currents
soaring heights
resting in
infinity of
air borne
seeing all
that is possible
then diving
directly into the beaks
of the boobies
snatching a fresh meal

Iwas, the Hawaiian name for frigate birds have a way of stealing food from other sea birds like the blue and red footed boobies.

Cake of the Wild

Layer cake with cardinal chirps
made of glitter, hope

Rooster crows doused in bruised egoes
shama calls dusted of dreams
with long tails

Zebra dove cooings waking
rising of imagination

Owl eyes decorating for perfect
night vision sometimes even used in the day

Mejiro feathers flashing yellow
lighting candles for all birthdays
even unbirthdays

The Plants

Wind Talk

Green fronds
loose
in breeze
like
flags waving
seem
to say keep
dancing
with me in
wind
keep shaking
off
the dust

Seed Spell

Simmering soil
shimmering seeds
a wakefulness
in sunlight
cascading angles
painted shade
from trees
and tall shrubs
beckoning for
newness, not what was
known, but for the rare
and subtle, like spells
cast into soil with worm
casings and the like
leaf flakes, old bones
and what has been buried
before simmering this soil

Guava Gold

The bark of guava
tree smooth like marble
fruits yellow gold and pink
on the inside with seeds
like flat droplets
the fruit flies so love this
they plant their eggs inside
must check fruit before taking a bite
unless you don't mind a little extra
protein, perhaps this the reason
why my son loves to eat his gold fruit
on the green side, a little less sweet
yet maggot free
when these yellow orbs
fall to earth, pigs, chickens, even worms
feast on golden delight

Footprints

His footprints on her footprints
she carrying the large bucket,
he pulling his dump truck on a string
big brother dancing on ahead,
wielding a stick chasing the roosters
growing fast legs,

Heading out to the new garden bed
to plants seeds,
I hope the cardinals don't
eat the seeds,

I hope the rose beetles, leave
the cotyledons emerging alone

I hope the chickens stay
out of the
new garden bed

Velvet on Earth

Though some much tougher
than velvet, the grasses,
buffalo, guinea, cane,
the one that smells like vanilla,
nut, pampas, bamboo,
each one different

Some grow taller than a queen,
some lay down roots stronger than
the heaviest elephants,
some have prickly hairs that
like to sew into the skin

All have edible new shoots sweet
with sugars merged from earth and sun
melted with water
some strong like a forest of love
you can fall into them laughing
feeling their embrace

Some have strong fibers you can
twiddle between your finger and thumb

then whistle a note to wake up the child inside
some have long stalks attracting flocks of
chestnut mannikins swooping
like swarms of bees
to feast on seeds of sunlight

Some so thick and fibrous kids make catapults
and arrows to shoot over the hill,
some strong as wood- timber bamboo,
to build outdoor kitchens, teepees and barns,
and some as fine as velvet skin upon the earth-

We mow the grass, weed whack it
watch it overtake the gardens, do our best to
manage it, and still, it is always our ally

Our velvet on earth,
to walk on, fall into, eat, play and feed to
our animal allies

The Beauty of Coconuts

I don't know if it is the milk
the coconut cream, or the meat,
or because they grow sky high
see many shades of green in this tree
the Hawaiians brought them
as staple food, and to weave
baskets and the like-
to climb a coconut tree-can feel
like rising to the height of a small mountain,
using a machete to crack open a nut-
like being a warrior gardener,
drinking coconut milk, the juice-
you can feel like queen of the garden

Tumeric

Olena, the Hawaiians call it,
golden root in the earth,
sending up large green
fleshy leaves, smelling spicy,
ten months in the soil,
then golden orange fingerlings
ready to be born from the dirt

Curry, chai tea, natural medicine
for just about anything,
some plants worth planting and praying for—
this, for sure one of those

Tapioca

Cassava, manioc, mandioca, yucca
manihot esculenta,
the white pearls in the box
mom used to cook with
milk, egg, and sugar
to make tapioca pudding, yum!

What does it really look like?

Big potato tubers in the ground
long red stem rising up with
pale green fingered leaves,
the roots a favorite of the wild pigs

Who would've known those
little white pearls come from
a big ole root from the ground
that must be cooked to be eaten

I never could turn the tapioca potato
shapes into little white pearls like
Bob's Red Mill could.

Lilikoi

First time seeing the flower
I wondered had it come from outer space,
exotic joy, these flowers cast a spell on me
sent me seeking the tropics

White petals leaning back
opening to purple and white spaghetti
curly cues, yellowish stamens shaped
like modern mini mop heads

With greenish pistols shaped flowercopters
I still don't understand how this flower
creates such tasty fruit- ova, bright yellow
when broken open see brilliant orange
sweet and sour seeds

The brilliance of nature astounding!

Apple Bananas

These bananas,
not like the Williams-
flashy yellow
at the supermarket,
not long, and overly sweet, soft,
these ones, fleshy,
deep yellow tones,
power packed tart with
just enough sweet,
eat them and feel like
the garden loves you

I had never tasted a different kind of banana until I moved to the tropics. Apparently the Hawaiians used to have over 200 different kinds of bananas!

Squash Stomping

Tall buffalo grass
covering the squash can't see
stomp feet to find squash

This became a favorite pastime when my sons were young, and
ready to help in the garden—squash stomping.

The Quest for Dark Leafy Greens

The quest for dark leafy greens
the kale, the collards, tatsoi, cilantro
or mizuna? or perennial chaya-
though those little tiny hairs,
seem to have a charge,
the katok, or parsley, edible hibiscus, or try a new one
noni leaf well cooked, which ones
shall come to the dinner table, stew or salad?
too bad my dad can't have dark leafy greens,
messes with his medications so he has to eat
orange, yellow or red, but not the green

Miracle fruit from the Miracle tree

I don't know how it does it,
when you eat some bites of the tiny fruit
and then you taste a sour lemon
the lemon tastes sweet like an overripe grape

Weaving Green

Tightly woven
vines holding
shape of mulberry
tree muffled
in green

Free this tree
let it be

Morning glory lines
weaving fine through
wire fence tender
hearts race in and out
to the top to

Reach
the light

Runner beans running wild
winding round pomegranate tree
back, side, front round
and round again and again

Spiraling to
find the highest light

Artistree

Wefts and wafts
for hats, baskets,
backpacks, toys,
even shelters
crafted from leaflets
of coconut fronds
green for so long
turning tan then brown
yet still holds fast, strong
steady as she blows
this coconut
tree herself a wonder

For the Love of Comfrey

Fuzzy leaves,
who could not love what you do
in the days of yore
your name, "bone knit"
I saw you knit my foot
back together this week

Ground roots blended
with tumeric, cayenne
painted on my foot
herbal magic not easy to understand
plant talks to body,
weaves cells together

These things I believe my grandmother
would have shared with me
if we had walked in the same garden

Kalo

Heart shaped, deep green leaves repel water,
loves to grow in moving water,
tuber nourishing people, pigs, chickens
fermenting makes even flavor stronger,
best when pounded to stew in juices making poi
feed to young babies as first food

Just to be sure, must cook on fire, boil
or place in underground oven
while the moon roams the sky
lest oxalic crystals of plant
create challenges in belly
fire in mouth or throat

Believed to have greatest life force of all foods
by Hawaiians, from sky father and earth mother
kalo fields, beautiful terracing,
sacred beloved plant

Kalo is the Hawaiian word for the plant taro.

Papaya

Exotic fleshy orange pear shape
slice in half see peppery seeds
like capers, shape size color

Perfect for breakfast,
shower with lemon juice,

When green, not ripe,
sap medicine for stings from bees,
or centipedes

Or use active enzymes
to clean the laundry,

Maybe pick green, and pickle papaya then share
and hear conversations about the delicious
pickled what?

Papaya—it can entice ya
really for all hearts to see

Sweet Potatoes

Purple, white or orange
these vines take over the entire
ground floor setting tubers
for the whole village
wait four months, then
cook up with coconut milk,
and replant all the leaves, what's
not to like about this Hawaiian sweet potato

Uala

Mango Season

For the sweetness that be-
a curse and a blessing,
from the family of Anacardiaceae,
 (poison oak, ivy)
urushiol the name of the poison that be

Only let lips touch the inner fruit
lest the sap drip on skin and create raised bumps,

Enjoy the inner flavor of mango under the skin,
and let the sap be just where it is, not on me

Rollinia Deliciosa

Sweet as sugar cane
shaped like a small yellow dragon
equipped with spikes
they're not real, just looks tough
with sun colored armor
protecting its delicate tender pulp,
messy yummy eat,
best eat with fingers,
slippery dark seeds slip to the side
feel the sweetness go inside
I see how it got its name
rollinia deliciosa

Night Blooming

Jasmine
how can it be?
by day feel your dainty
quiet demure,
small tender white flowers
against your flourishing
shiny green
humble, soft whisper

By eve your
hardy vociferous exotic self
perfumes the air
waking me up to
remember stars intoxicating

The night life of moths
seek your pollen
your realm of life
more alive
in the sensual sensing
of the night

Ginger Queen

Fire of subterranean
warming my heart
my soul
no doubt feminine
consciousness rising into river
of life

Sipping her tea
two fat fingers in a gallon
of h2o
thin slices simmering for
twenty to thirty charms
lava like flavor
earth moving
pouring into me

golden tubers layering in the aina
multiply adorning green
feathers atop to catch wind
and harvest fresh light all around

Burrowing through red brown crumbles
fingerlings reach forward
into tunnels of time
tasting the stories woven into soil

No small matter to drink
flame woven from dusty dirt
droplets of sunshine, the fire in my belly
growing wisdom into
the fiber of my being

Fire rising
ginger queen

Aina is Hawaiian word for the land which feeds us.

Garden Notes

Kinky hose
stopping flow
unkink hose
watch the flow
holes on leaves
small green
'pillars, pick them
or let wasps get'em
gray lit day
keep water at bay
sun over by
let hose on high

It Comes with the Farm

Along with red dirt, critters, and the dynamics of the place
all this "life" comes with the farm

Red Dirt

This carpet of red earth draping
over our planet's face
holds fast to the roots,
iron colored
staining
under fingernails,
soles of feet, toes and
smudge on face,
shirt has stains
shorts as well,
oh well,
we can tell
barefoot day,
farm clothes OK

Mosquito Season

Swat them
smoke them
pinch them
blow them
squish them
trap them
smash them
just don't
feed them
or breed them
and
stand in the sun
dance in the rain
run in the wind
put your face near the fire
to feel the relief

The Ants

Come marching, all sizes and shapes,
some with wings, some can jump,
all carry more than their own weight,
walk in long lines, acting clean up crew
looking for water, looking for leftovers-
small snacks for the mighty,
don't care if they're in house, garden, or tree,
they'll nest where ever they please,
carry their dead, scout for the wounded,
thanks for eating those termites,
they bug me even more,
can you please just stay out of the honey jar?

Lizard Self

Lizard lips face the sun
eyes roll round and
wispy tongue tastes the dawn
while scaly skin spikes the air, yet,
shedding skin again and again,

Wearing armor
or not wearing armor
maybe time to shed again,

Serpentine movement, crawl not walk
slithery tongue peak, not speak
eyes span land with forever tongue
tasting air, finding food, water, safety, shelter
changing color here and there,

Fierce dinosaur tail
cold blood in soil-- means
heart beat slow, groove move,
not move, groove, not move
hunting style walking up trees
into the fire of the day

Love Note to Bee

Not just because of your honey
or your propolis
or your sweet buzz or fuzz

Nor because I love watching you
pollinating flowers

Nor because of your masterful
hives, dripping in sweet magnificence,
geometric wizardry

Nor because of your over fifty million
years of presence on the planet

Maybe because even though you can sting
I feel love and safety around you in the garden

Please continue to thrive despite the poor choices
made in corporate thought in your world garden

You are necessary
you are love
please continue to be
bee

Free Range

Free range
a concept we adore, free range the birds, the cats,
the goats, the dogs, the plants, the kids galore

Only to discover
we trespass onto one another,
and the piles get messy,
because chickens and geese
like to stand by the front door,
and so do their stories of all that they ate

And the goats will just go where they please,
even if the new tree just planted is free to grow with ease

Children make ramps and tree houses and forts,
this I can handle, so they get to be free

However in the end, for all the rest of above, I adore
all the cages, all the fences to lock out and lock into
their places, each to their own
the animals, plants, and nosy neighbors

The Night Sounds

Katydids the loudest, their sounds grace time,
cheering more loudly when teeming together
as if they have won the game,
a continuous piercing whistling drowning
all thoughts into mighty one,

Grasshoppers, of the short horned and long horned,
I can't tell which, and perhaps they are different,
one day find out,
chirps smile into the night, their rhythms
guiding lullabies to the heart

The small tree frogs the sweetest,
 generally I hear one alone,
and wonder how patience must pay off

Bullfrogs galumph, the bass of the crowd,
the deep sounds, with rhythm, and force boisterous
loud the evening air rich, with the sounds of
this orchestra, night tones, warm bravado

Singing out the day and
blurring into the stars

Ready to Run

Out of an egg, small crack breaks baby gecko free
born fully ready to run
tiny dragon, fingers gripping seeking
with perfect sharp vision, and belly breathing
a place to land hidden
lizard feet grip the moment to stick to the table
upside down now
run from playful kitten now biting
wiggling tail while the rest
of little gecko running now tail free

Night Rain

On balmy warm nights, when cloud cover strong,
humidity rises, and those raindrops must fall
ringing of droplets on tin roof above
can wake me with oh so sweet kisses of rain
a moment of electricity, generally magical
except for the year where it rained for forty days
and forty nights, a galloping endless herd
of heavy pounding hooves on roof, sounding like
coconuts continuously falling to earth
making us jumpy and tired and wet everyday
I prefer the gentle persuasion of raindrops like lover

Tropic Grey

Oh the rains
when fine mist shifts
to pounding fury
contouring shapes
carving into pathways

When rivers pour from
rain gutters, leap tips, tree limbs,
old stones

Light turns grey
grey turns black in day lack
saving time
whose time?

Rain time

Out doors seeking indoors
sunshine begging to climb in the windows
to shiver off the grey

Winter dawns in tropic grey
sing in the sun
sing in the day
oh where do the birds hide now?

Outdoor Kitchen

Timber bamboo spiraling upwards, holding
frame, steadying shelter, touching sky,
oh this kitchen edifice magnificence

We cook rice in open elements receiving
protection from rain, though rats, mice
visit and birds fly through,

Chickens, geckoes, beetles, mosquitoes
meander in while lazy farm dog, cats
rest in sun forgetting to guard the cookery

Come on sun's up wake up!
wash everything before cooking
paw prints in pans, some dribbles in plates

Did the shama make the nest again
in the hanging pot? Doesn't she know
cats love to watch her babies grow
tell me shama do you see them as friend or foe?

Shucking coconut in bamboo round room
listening to bird song, breeze song

Tea kettle whistling as smells of
flowering orange tree lingers in air
making food taste like
we must lick our fingers

Blown

When a bird gets blown across oceans
through storms through veils
of sea wind and time
it arrives un-tropical, hungry,
wind blown, still feathered
then land, life and water
feed, nourish, warm
revealing tenacity of spirit
in a soul of a bird blown
from its regularly scheduled meals

The Magic of Urine

Some see it as waste,
tree sees it as nourishment, we know from our
once avocado seedling, receiving daily buckets
of urine steeping in sawdust, douse with water in soil
around baby tree with hose, daily

Imagine our surprise when three years later,
this once seed, now tree, now fruiting beauty
gifts us our first avocado, beautiful round shape,

We now know how to speed a seed into tree
growth comes with might and
a touch of the color yellow

After Storm

Dots of leaves scatter landscape, bent rain gutter, skyward roots
of eucalyptus, muddy trails, piles, waterway groove, large branches
inhabit pathways, upside down patio chairs scratch in air, dead rat,
running cockroaches, grass now marshland, twisted tarps, tired earth worms,
barely bird songs, shake laundry geckoes fly out, towels hung flung in dirt,
appreciating peace in sun, now quiet winds, like a cough gone missing,
this calm after the storm

Why Does the Orchid

Why does the orchid like to suffer?
do all epiphytes fight for water?
fight to squeeze droplets out of air?
do they drink through a straw,
each rootlet?
and when they blossom in beauty
can they rest and see the world
through the flowering
or must they still fight
to find invisible rain?

Sounds of Hunger

In silence
this afternoon,
they arrive ready
to feed barely fledglings
waddling in nests nearby.

Their high whistle dancing,
pierces soundscape breaking stillness,
mejiros-brilliant yellow
with keen white dots accenting eyes,
beaks comb through hibiscus bush
finding a meal hidden within vault of green
like parrotfish crunching through coral reef

Suddenly, more abrupt, shrill peeps
with sharpness of mothers
shrieking to scold monsters,
a quickening of sounds and feathers,
see flying yellows dart like fearful
squid flying through brushy undercurrents

Underneath hibiscus hedge,
mini lion stalking, following
chitter and chatter then
pouncing, raising shrill volume
of mother birds- feathers fly,
sounds get louder, then
with feathered mouth
small lion slinks away

Truly empty bellies
Have ears for
sounds of hunger

Hurricane Season

Louder now with this electronic age
phone calls to wake you pull
you out of bed for warnings
of storms flash floods and the like

And if the big one comes
I have seen from photos- roofs on houses peal
off like the top of a can opening by can opener
coconut trees shredding like lettuce for a salad

Spare us

Spare us this season
let us be well to keep
sinking roots into
the earth for a spell
thank you, thank you, thank you
dear mother nature

Where Dragonflies Sleep

In calm of night
light breeze sweeps
sounds of crickets into channels,
spaces under leaves where
dragonflies sleep

Breathe in to touch heart,
breathe out to reach for starlight
beckoning from depths beyond the beyond

Luminescent veil thinning dimensions,
merging formless, wordless feelings bridging heartbeats to
reach through portals into realms of those traveling before

Listen, listen for song, meaning, colors, feelings, dreams,
speaking, symbols weaving

This language, this essence, before time
let it merge into heart
let this beacon touch you like
sunlight warms you

Christmas Crescendo

From the south came
strong hungry winds
chasing confetti leaves
leaving scattered greens
over ground over dale
this morning

Mourn tree branches snapped
hanging like ornaments
some uprooted sixty footers
offerings for this Christmas

Christmas power booming
from storm winds rain
as sun starts to shine light onto
plants who gave their lives this season

Seasoning of remembering
like salt and pepper give every meal
a Christmas tree gives every season its life
life force crescendo of a storm reminds us to
honor the trees in this giving time

Cats' Eyes

Seamless shades of blue to indigo to black
late dusk chasing away the sun
see the stars turn on, like cats' eyes
shining onto earth

Night sky yowling all these
meows in the sky
looking at me wondering why
I haven't had a beach fire in a while
why there are no embers left
to twinkle back, to wink at you

Twinkle twinkle
little cats
how I wonder
where you're at
up above the
world so high
I like your
freedom
in the sky

Kudos to Woofers

Those who touched
the plants, the earth
the animals,
our hearts,
the cycles,
willing workers on organic farms-
aka "woofer"

Each one touching us
in some way,
weeding, building,
planting, composting,
harvesting, digging, driving,
clearing, burying, sawing,
engaging children, singing,
watering, feeding,

Efforts helping the family farm
to grow and thrive,
some, still young,
threw tantrums at work,
not knowing how to show up
and yet,

Still did contribute
in ways,
teaching us how to
be better humans
to not throw tantrums back

Gifts of pottery,
kindness, stories,
music, fun, laughter,
farm work, farm fun
seeing people working together

In harmony,
growing plants,
raising animals,
raising children
brings a certain kind
of warmth to my heart

I cannot find in cities, nor
car rides, nor schools,
so kudos to all woofers,
making a difference
in the world!

Night Wind

Shivering palms
shake like rattles
bullfrogs boom
on backside of
wind beyond a caress
raking through
contours of earth,
leafs flippant
flop flap
sounds like static
stuck between
radio stations
night wind
churning in my mind
wanting sleep yet
night wind uplift
leaves in my soul
leaving none unturned

So What Exactly is Permaculture?

May not look like much to you this messy garden
weeds running amok the kale and tatsoi
however flowers of this weed attract the beneficials,
lady bugs and wasps –ones who keep vigilance
over caterpillars and baby grasshoppers
eating dark leafy greens

Penned by Bill Mollison and Dave Holmgren
after spending time in natural landscapes
then mimicking nature layering landscape
on a farm, making a "permanent agricultural system"
permaculture harmoniously integrating
landscape and people with sustainability at roots

It's all about relationship
it's all about respect
care of earth-and all life systems,

Why is the tree towering over the
funny looking bean?
she is madre de cacao, mother of chocolate

guarding her cacao, tree giving shade
protection as chocolate grows
sweetly in shadow of mama gliricidia

We welcome worms, toads, wasps do sting,
but carry off caterpillars, even centipedes help
as long as they live in the garden
though, please don't come in the house

How did that beautiful small hill get there?
oh, the hugelkultur? the place where we buried
bent spoons, broken buckets, rotten 2 x 4s,
piles of sticks, tennis shoes that flap,
cardboard, large logs, pillows with no life,
and the like, then covered with soil
planting trees atop, basically
we threw and grew

When we mulch, how muchling wild chickens
love the mulching they kick and spray
all mulch away, till bare naked sits the soil
around new trees layer coconut fronds
on top of mulch pile, when hens come to dig,
leaflets bind round ankles

– now no more kung fu chickens kicking straw
Community plantings, as seen in forests layers,
moss, ferns, mushrooms at ground floor,
when conditions just right
perfect humidity and temp, naturally
invite layering of herbs, low plants,
small trees then large trees, then over story

Forest garden story

Thank you Mr. Mollison
for your love of nature, humans,
bright mind and sharing
may you rest in eternal garden of peace

Cycles of Abundance

Sunshine, rain, mud, mangoes
rooster calls, night rain, light breezes, *weeds*
fresh air, goats, goat scat, goat milk
kids, worms, papayas, *weeds*
sugar cane, wild chickens, greens, smiles
bananas, lilikois, noni, pigs, *weeds*
sour grass, well water, eggs, gotu kola
avocadoes, lemons, kittens, *weeds*
hono hono, guinea grass, hila hila, far off stars,
longons, beans, rats, cockroaches, *weeds*,
cricket songs, compost, rose beetles, fleas
lice, shama birds, cabbage butterflies, *weed*s
jaboticabas, plumerias, rollinia deliciosa, *weeds*,
miracle fruits, myna birds, abeyus, *weeds*
sunshine, rain...

Day this Night

They sing with such power
calling forth spring in this dark
rhythmic chirping spilling into mine ears
laconic this wind, this night waking up
falling stars, these crickets whose cup of
notion seems day this night

Fresh Luminescence

Pearl drops from sky
essence of wet light from nigh

Receive all this moisture
makes lighter the green
deeper the roots
flowers they shine

When sky goes from
dark grey and then
back to blue

Scent of raw soil
trill of the cardinal
song of the shama
fly high to the sky

Spaces

With eyes
oblique, peripheral

See

Innuendos, nuances,
subtle clues and cues

Written in invisible ink
between words, letters, breaths

Betwixt fingers,
cloud spans, constellations

And if you read only
the spaces in between

You just might find a thread
leading to a spacious
inner sanctum

G'night

Half moon smiles
cat purring in my
face wind churning palm
leaves stirring the night
cauldron singing frogs
sending spells of unspent kisses
into pond of dreams
layering thoughts and wishes
to bake this enchanted
black folding eve

If you read a poem and feel your own nature connection, you have made me smile.

ABOUT THE AUTHOR

Sumi Yamauchi finds every poem has a soul, an essence best expressed through connecting to nature.

As an empath, animal lover, mother, gardener, dancer, artist, she enjoys bringing words from unspoken forms of life into poetry.

She sees this truth of connection to oneself and nature living at the root of all meaningfully spoken, like tapping into an ancient connection breathing words into existence.

She writes from her farm home on the island of Kauai.

Learn more at: *www.poetreebird.com*

www.ingramcontent.com/pod-product-compliance
Lightning Source LLC
Chambersburg PA
CBHW020204090426
42734CB00008B/931